Praise for
The Youthful Midlife Traveller
A Baby Boomer's Guide to Independent World Travel

"A lot of great information that isn't overwhelming." - Terry T

"Chris gives it to you straight, cold, hard truth about the challenges inherent in global travel. Very helpful to me, as I'm planning a trip around the world. And since he's already travelled around the globe, I know his words come from direct experience, which is exceptionally helpful. I liked the safety, social, items to pack and all other recommendations. I like that he recommends alternatives and explains them in detail so you can be aware of your own best choices. A very detailed and informative guide and resource to complete a global travel excursion." - Jennifer Z

"I liked the guide overall." - Steve M

"As a solo traveller I learned some tips I am going to implement in my future travels. Lots of good information. I like the overall theme - get out there and experience life, whether it's a big solo trip or a small jaunt to get you started. Good information for people just starting out as well as for those who have more experience. I like that you make people aware of pitfalls and that issues will come up but if one stays calm and thinks clearly there is always a solution. I feel that is very important for people to understand - something will inevitably happen; it's how one deals with it that will determine how your attitude towards travel plays out. With the personal experiences adding reality to it is helpful and could give first time travellers a sense of comfort. Love the idea behind it and that you want to encourage people to just get out there and live!" - Jackie T

"I enjoyed your guide." - Ken L

"Very thorough and in depth." - Joanie S

"This is an EXCELLENT guide. I'm truly impressed at the content, quality, and value you deliver." - Gary W

The Youthful Midlife Traveller

A Baby Boomer's Guide to Independent World Travel

Chris Herrmann

Copyright © 2023 by Chris Herrmann.

All rights reserved. No part of this book may be used or reproduced in any form whatsoever without written permission except in the case of brief quotations in critical articles or reviews.

Printed in Australia, USA.

For more information, or to book an event, contact:
chrish@myseniorgapyear.com
http://www.myseniorgapyear.com

ISBN - Print: 978-0-6485222-6-3
ISBN - eBook : 978-0-6485222-7-0

First Edition: November 2023

CONTENT

INTRODUCTION 1

YOUR TRAVEL STYLE 7

    Chapter 1 Types of Travel 7

    Chapter 2. Purpose 17

    Chapter 3 Myths of Travel 23

    Chapter 4. Fears 31

    Chapter 5 Your Travel Style Summary 37

PLANNING YOUR ADVENTURE 41

    Chapter 6 Choosing Your Destination 41

    Chapter 7 Research Destinations 45

    Chapter 8 Getting There 49

    Chapter 9 Getting Around 55

    Chapter 10 Accommodation 61

    Chapter 11 Travel Insurance 67

    Chapter 12 Visas 71

    Chapter 13 Health & Immunisations 75

    Chapter 14 Documents & Checklist 81

    Chapter 15 Planning Your Adventure Summary 85

TRAVEL SMARTS 89

    Chapter 16 Solo Travelling 89

    Chapter 17 Earning an Income While Travelling 93

    Chapter 18 Travelling Longer Is Cheaper 97

    Chapter 19 Travel Smarts Summary 99

TRAVEL ESSENTIALS **101**

    Chapter 20 What to Pack 101

    Chapter 21 Cash and Credit Cards 105

    Chapter 22 Managing Your Money 109

    Chapter 23 Technology 113

    Chapter 24 Social 117

    Chapter 25 Activities 121

    Chapter 26 How to Travel Safely 125

    Chapter 27 Travel Essentials Summary 129

LIVING LIKE A LOCAL **133**

    Chapter 28 Why Live Like a Local 133

    Chapter 29 Living Like a Local 137

    Chapter 30 Living Like a Local Summary 141

KEEPING YOUR DREAM ALIVE **143**

ABOUT THE AUTHOR **147**

RESOURCES **151**

RESOURCES
Throughout the book are references to Resources. This is an online comprehensive list of added resource information. This includes links and video interviews of other independent travellers. See the Resources section at the end of the book.

INTRODUCTION

Welcome and congratulations on joining The Youthful Midlife Travellers - for youthfully minded Boomers!

I'm excited and delighted to share with you my experiences and tips, as well as insights from other travel experts.

What a fantastic stage of life where we can travel! There has never been a better time in history to explore the world. With a wider choice of flights and extensive low-cost communication, the far reaches of the globe are now more accessible than ever.

So, what does it mean to be a Youthful Midlife Traveller for a youthfully minded Boomer? To me, it means:
- Experiencing new destinations and incredible natural wonders,
- Embracing different cultures and meeting amazing people along the way,

THE YOUTHFUL MIDLIFE TRAVELLER

- Traveling in a way that allows you to choose your own itinerary and decide on tours and activities as you go,
- All of this with the added benefit of the experience and maturity that this stage in life brings, but with an adventurous and youthful mindset!

Visiting destinations like Machu Picchu, nestled high in the Andes Mountains of Peru, exploring the Amazon, the world's largest tropical rainforest, or immersing yourself in the wonders of the Galapagos Islands - these are just a few examples of what you can experience as a youthfully minded Youthful Midlife Traveller.

A Bit About Myself
As a world traveller, author, and speaker, I've been exploring the globe for over 47 years, venturing into some 46 countries. More recently, I embarked on an exciting twelve-month solo backpacking gap year adventure around the world, covering 23 countries. After returning from my senior gap year, I wanted to share my experiences to help inspire others to live their travel dreams.

The story of **My Senior Gap Year** has been published in both English and Chinese, drawing interest from the BBC and numerous TV, radio, print, and online media outlets across Australia, the USA, Europe, and Asia. I have been invited to share my story at various organizations.

The Youthful Midlife Travellers guide also draws on the experiences of other world travellers, including valuable advice from experienced solo traveling women.

Why This Guidebook?
There are numerous benefits to being a Youthful Midlife Traveller. Apart from staying active, research supports the idea this type of travel stimulates the aging brain. It can also be a more cost-effective way to explore the world.

It's not just practical; it's also fun. While immersing ourselves in other cultures can be challenging, it can also be immensely rewarding and exhilarating. We now have more options at our disposal - from more comfortable travel choices to a more down-to-earth and adventurous approach. It's our choice, and you get to cherish the freedom it provides. That's why I'm thrilled to share this guide with you.

My message is simple: don't wait for an ideal time in the future. Start living your dreams now, even if it's just by taking one small step toward your travel goal. Don't be the one to regret putting off what you could have done.

What's Included in the Guide?
This guide will walk you through the 7 steps on How to be a Youthful Midlife Traveller as a youthfully minded Boomer. The guide is designed not only to share the "how" but also to find our purpose for traveling. Let's be honest here - we are

THE YOUTHFUL MIDLIFE TRAVELLER

creatures of habit, and we often get stuck in our comfort zones. Our dreams can be overshadowed by our fears. I understand these doubts - what if this happens, what if that, am I too old? But remember, people just like you and me are currently enjoying the experience of being a Youthful Midlife Traveller. So why not you?

Whether you are new to independent travel or an experienced traveller looking to take it to the next level, it's your turn to start or elevate your journey.

The book is divided into several sections:
- **Your Travel Style**: This section helps you clarify your preferred style and purpose of travel, dispelling myths and addressing common concerns that might be holding you back.

- **Planning Your Adventure**: Here, we cover all the essentials of planning your adventure, from selecting destinations and booking flights to arranging accommodations, securing travel insurance, obtaining visas, and organizing your trip.

- **Travel Smarts**: This section explores smart travel strategies, including solo travel, ways to travel longer on a budget, and even earning an income while travelling.

- **Travel Essentials**: We delve into the practical aspects of travelling, such as what to pack, managing your finances, and making the most of your time upon arrival. The fun really begins at this stage as we look at making social connections, activities to engage in, financial survival tips, and ensuring your safety.

- **Living Like a Local**: Discover the benefits of the ultimate cultural immersion experience - living like a local.

- **Keeping Your Dream Alive**: Perhaps the most important step, this section discusses how to keep your dream alive. It's easy to have big ideas, but what do we need to do to ensure they become more than just fleeting thoughts?

No matter where you are in your travel journey, whether you're completely new or seeking to expand your level of travel experience, I hope this guide will enlighten you at each step, giving you the knowledge and confidence to explore the exciting opportunities that being a Youthful Midlife Traveller offers. Above all, I want you to feel empowered to have the courage to live your travel dreams.

THE YOUTHFUL MIDLIFE TRAVELLER

YOUR TRAVEL STYLE

Chapter 1
Types of Travel

It's time to start turning our dreams into reality. We need to consider our preferred style of travel. Do you prefer luxury, a more down-to-earth travel adventure, or to travel like a local?

The exciting thing about being an independent global traveller is you get to choose your style of travel. Travel encompasses a broad range of experiences. At one end are the "flop and drop" relaxation getaways, such as luxury resorts, beach bungalows, cruises, etc. There's the fully organized tour where everything is planned for you. Organized tours can also offer a range of tours with a more adventurous experience, catering to various preferences. There are also higher-risk physical endurance adventure experiences, which may be part of a tour package or undertaken as an independent traveller.

In between all these options is my preferred travel style: low-risk travel that emphasizes adventurous cultural experiences. As an independent global traveller, you decide the mix of experiences that suits you.

Let's briefly delve into some of these main options in more detail.

1. Flop and Drop Holidays
I categorize this as a vacation rather than traveling. The advantage is that it offers total relaxation without the need for much planning, except maybe whether to swim, eat, or drink. As an independent traveller, this restful experience can be a welcome R&R if you are traveling for an extended period. During my year of traveling, I used time on idyllic islands as the perfect opportunity for rest and

relaxation!

2. Organized Tour

One of the benefits of an organized tour is everything is done for you. The only planning you need to do is deciding which tour company and which tour to join. It offers a very social experience with other travellers. If you are new to travel or just venturing out on your own, joining a tour can be an excellent way to get your feet wet. Even experienced travellers will often use a tour to become familiar with an unfamiliar country before returning as an independent traveller.

I posed that question to Helen, an experienced solo world traveller on her advice to others thinking about solo travelling: *"...try a small tour by themselves. So, can they manage on their own on a small tour? And then maybe, after that, they do something by themselves."*

Jackie had similar advice: *"I went to Morocco, and everybody's like, you shouldn't go to Morocco. So, the first trip I went to Morocco. I did it as a tour. I booked a tour, and I was there for two weeks in December and loved it, fell in love with Morocco, and realized very quickly that* you could do this as a solo woman, although people recommend you don't. You absolutely could do it as a solo woman."

See Resources for full interviews with Helen & Jackie.

3. Totally Free Independent Travel

As a Totally Free Independent Traveller, you do everything yourself – from planning your itinerary, booking your own accommodation, transport, etc. You organize all your tours. The benefit of this as a totally free independent traveller is you are in control of absolutely everything and have complete flexibility over your itinerary. You are entirely on your own. With this form of travel, you must decide the level of risk you are personally comfortable with. For example, if your itinerary takes you to places that are too isolated, it can be more challenging if things go wrong, such as dealing with sickness.

4. Youthful Midlife Traveller

As a Youthful Midlife Traveller, you still organize your itinerary and choose the style of experiences, but you may also add in short, guided tours along the way. On arrival at a destination, you may decide to use a local tour or guide, whether for a day or the duration of your stay. I often use the local walking tour of a city to familiarize myself when I first arrive at a place. For certain popular attractions, you cannot go unless you hire a tour guide. In other situations, language may make it too limited without a bilingual guide. A guide may be a private guide or part of a group. In most cases, you can arrange a guide at the destination. People in travel groups, such as Facebook travel groups, can often provide a good source of recommendations. To me, this form of travel is not about personal adventurous risk but about adventurous cultural experiences.

In less popular tourist destinations or regions where I am not as familiar, I will generally travel only on common tourist routes. That way, you always have access to the resources of other travellers for safety reasons, and if emergency situations arise. Central America is an example. It's not overcrowded with tourists, but it's popular enough to have well-established tourist routes where you do not have to be isolated. Each town I visited had an ample supply of businesses selling bus tickets on popular tourist routes. Unless you want to be a pioneer explorer, the world offers many cultural experiences, without

THE YOUTHFUL MIDLIFE TRAVELLER

being overly commercialized.

Booking as you go spreads the booking time over the whole trip. The advantage is if you like a place, you can stay longer, and if not, you can move on. It also removes what otherwise can seem like a huge job of preplanning and booking the whole itinerary before you go. However, if you are traveling as a group of friends, I would suggest that such flexibility could be tested!

My aim is to take a step away from the over-commercialized tourist destinations. Valencia in Spain is another example. Yes, there are tourists, but it's a far cry from the ever-popular Barcelona. And I believe it offers a more accessible and authentic cultural experience as a result. That's the key difference for an independent traveller. You don't need to follow the crowd. Popular tourism is where everyone goes. But with crowds, it's harder to access more authentic experiences. Plus, you'll be paying double the cost for the experience.

You may also choose to enjoy some well-deserved pampering within your trip, such as a short cruise or a stay at a resort. At another stage of your trip, you may look for more physical adventure like a challenging hike or a short kayaking expedition. It's your choice. You choose. You are in control and to the level your budget allows.

Less is More
Another key issue is how much time you wish to travel. This, of course, depends on your commitments, which may include dependencies such as children, aging parents, work, finances, etc. We will cover the cost of travel later, including how the longer you can travel, the cheaper it is, down to as affordable as traveling on a pension. With a more flexible itinerary, the more you can be open to new opportunities and experiences, the more you'll potentially experience those unexpected memorable times.

The idea of traveling solo for 12 months was initially daunting for me. I was going to break it up and come home halfway through. I'm glad I didn't as it added to the whole unique experience. If the idea appeals to you but you don't feel you are ready, start with small baby step trips to build your confidence. We will cover more on solo traveling later.

Here's an important factor to consider. It's a huge world. It is impossible to expect we can fully experience every country in our lifetime. Sure, it is exciting visiting as many countries as you can, but it's also tiring and can become travel for travel's sake. Where it can become overwhelming with one mountain starting to look like another and another tropical beach the same as the last.

An alternative is to focus on more quality than quantity experiences. That is, choose fewer countries and become more absorbed in the cultural experience. It's also a less stressful way of traveling. You spend more time in a destination, which allows you to get involved in the community. You can then use that destination as a base to see other attractions.

People ask me what my most memorable experience was during my twelve-month gap year adventure. Backpacking from country to country was exciting. But probably the most memorable was basing myself in one place for 3 months. We'll cover more on this in the Live Like a Local Section.

Aging Brain Benefit
When choosing where you wish to travel and for how long, here's another very interesting consideration. According to research, engaging with a totally different culture offers significant mental health benefits for the aging brain. Travel presents new experiences that challenge just about all our senses. Stimulating our sight, smell, sounds, and touch. Maybe this explains why immersing yourself in a completely different culture, though challenging, at the same time, is such a very stimulating experience. Some research even goes as far as supporting that travel can contribute to a lower risk of later dementia.

Summary
In summary, consider the range of travel options. If you're new to independent travel, an organized tour can be an excellent way to become more familiar and, therefore, more confident in being more personally adventurous with your future travel plans. Limit how much you try to conquer seeing every corner of the world. Richer experiences can be more meaningful and rewarding.

Be bold with your plans.
"Freedom lies in being bold." — Robert Frost

THE YOUTHFUL MIDLIFE TRAVELLER

Chapter 2.
Purpose

They say a purposeful life is a good life. But does this need to apply when travelling? More than just exploring, travel can be a great way to be open to discovering new opportunities. Some of the most memorable experiences can come from having a completely open itinerary, open to finding unique experiences and then having the time to seize opportunities.

Before I left for my gap year, it frustrated me I was leaving with no purpose. It didn't seem meaningful, just traveling for travel's sake. In the end, I couldn't find a purpose and went anyway. Surprisingly, I came across several enriching, purposeful opportunities as I travelled, opportunities where I could give back.

Linen Project

One opportunity I felt extremely privileged to become involved with, then turned into a million-dollar charity benefiting people around the globe.

Such opportunities may not occur again, but no matter how big or small, opportunities are waiting for us if we are open to them. A significant contributing factor was I didn't feel constrained by a fixed itinerary, and I was therefore open to finding an opportunity.

Volunteering

Volunteering can be a wonderful way of giving back. The ultimate travel experience is connecting with local people. Volunteering can be an excellent way to achieve this. (See Resource for volunteer opportunities). There's a range of organizations that have evolved to meet this growing demand. Some have become quite commercialized. Personally, if I am working as a volunteer, I don't want to be paying thousands of dollars for a commercial enterprise's marketing and admin costs.

There are local organizations such as Rotary

International clubs all around the world where you can get involved with some of the overseas projects they support. Another example which wasn't pre-planned was a Rotary project in Nicaragua. This provided a very rich cultural experience during this stay.

Voluntourism, as it's often referred to, can be a trap, and you need to check who it benefits most – you as the tourist having a feel-good moment or the commercial organisation managing the recipient community. Ideally, there's a balance. In some cases, wasted money from foreign "do-good" projects have more of a detrimental effect on the receiving community.

Perspectives
Travel offers an opportunity to challenge your opinions and perspectives. I changed my view on a range of political and social issues such as terrorism, drug prohibition, and waste, simply by spending time and being open to appreciating the perspective of others, often with very different views.

THE YOUTHFUL MIDLIFE TRAVELLER

Interests

Travel can be an exciting way to discover new interests or re-establish old ones. What type of experience are you looking for? What do you want to gain personally? Do you want to expand your knowledge of history, architecture, culture, language, food, etc.? You may enjoy researching the area before you arrive or when you are there. Just being a part of and engaging within a different culture can be a primary motivation.

Empowerment

Perhaps you are seeking to build your sense of empowerment, a 'can do' attitude, building your confidence in undertaking something that is outside your comfort zone. This can be particularly relevant if you have experienced a significant life change such as retirement, empty nest, loss of a partner, etc. Traveling can help build a feeling of empowerment, offering a sense of achievement as well as having fun at the same time.

Relationships

For couples, travel can be an exciting way to rejuvenate a relationship. Research supports that when couples travel together, they create lasting shared experiences. While adventurous travel can be stressful, good stress means that couples are forced to work as a team. Couples can then look back and know that as a team, they collaborated to achieve their goal together. That's where shared experiences are fondly recalled.

Jo Wilson from The Relationship Rejuvenator said, *"research supports this time and time again that when couples travel together, they are creating shared experiences. So, when you're in a distressed environment, it is so beautiful, and then it's also wonderful to put your couple. Shift into stress as well, but good stress means that you're forced to work as a team."* (Hear more from Jo Wilson in Resources)

Summary
The purpose of your travel is individual. You may have a specific motive for travel, such as deepening your knowledge of history. It may be to give back through volunteering or to revitalize your relationship. Others, like me, may enjoy a more open structure to explore. What's your purpose? Is it open to explore, or do you have a defined goal?

THE YOUTHFUL MIDLIFE TRAVELLER

Chapter 3
Myths of Travel

There are many myths of travel that prevent people from traveling the world. Let's look at some of the main ones...

Cost

Ask people why they don't travel, and many will say they can't afford it. But by being smart about where, when, and how you travel, traveling the world can be as cost-effective as staying home. It's all about approaching your travel differently. We cover this later.

Before I left on my twelve-month trip around the world, a friend asked, "Wow, that must be costing you a fortune?" The reality was my whole year cost less than if I had lived in Australia. For longer-term travel, unless you need a five-star lifestyle, you can effectively swap your living expenses at home for travel expenses.

By choosing the right destination, there are many places that offer the feel of a five-star lifestyle on a low-cost travel budget.

Longer-term travel is a totally different experience from your short two-week vacation. On a short vacation, you can afford more expensive resort-style holidays. By comparison, traveling for longer periods means moderating your usual short-term daily travel budget to be more aligned with your normal living costs at home. As we progress through the guide, we'll be discussing in more detail a range of ways to travel more affordably.

Language
But I can't speak the language of the countries I am visiting, you might say. Well, neither could I as I travelled through Spain and Latin America. In fact, I went there knowing only two words of Spanish – Si & Que!

However, I believe it is important to know at least some basic greeting words and phrases. It shows respect when interacting with local people in the countries you visit. Some people will take on intensive language training in preparation for a trip. That's a great thing to do, but personally, it's not essential. From my experience, you can go anywhere in the world with the most basic phrases, and you will get by.

After all, we are all the same humans with the same needs and wants. We all appreciate being respected with a 'please' and 'thank you', 'have a nice day'. We basically eat the same food. Chicken is chicken the world over, vegetables, cheese, bread, wine, and beer. I was once in a restaurant in an isolated village in China. I had zero local language ability. But with the help of pictures and performing charade-like animations, we got by. Apps like Google Translate are a godsend. Though, of course, make sure you have mobile internet. More on that later. And yes, there are certainly big benefits in learning a language, which we will also discuss later.

Loneliness

You may also be concerned that being away on your own, you would feel too lonely. That is a valid concern. After all, we are social beings, and we need social contact. The thought of traveling solo, or even as a couple, and not engaging with other people can feel isolating. Organized tours or cruises are an easy choice where social needs are taken care of.

But just because you travel independently doesn't mean you miss out. People would ask me if I was ever lonely when I travelled solo for a year. It was the first time in my life I ever travelled solo. But the answer was no. Certainly, I was always conscious of being alone, but I never suffered the true feeling of loneliness. That's because I believe the world has changed so dramatically in our lifetime. Technology and communications have shrunk the world, making connecting with other people much simpler. Family is readily accessible through messages as well as video calls. On top of that, you really meet some fantastic people along the way, many of whom can become lifelong friends. We'll be discussing ways to make social contact when traveling later.

Bored

Being bored is not something you equate with travel. If you are constantly on the move, there is never-ending mental stimulation. But travel can be tiring and overwhelming and lead to burnout. The alternative is the "stop and smell the roses" approach where you stay in one place for much longer and become much more absorbed in the local community. For me, 1-3 months was an ideal time. It offers an experience more like living like a local. It is challenging but rewarding.

The concern many people have about staying in one place for an extended time is that they will get bored. Once again, technology has made this a huge game changer. A range of apps allow you to discover many activities you can connect with other people. I spent three months in Valencia in Spain. I arrived not knowing a soul, but by the time I left, I had a great little social group. Was I bored? No. In fact, my calendar was far busier compared to the previous year at home. And I thought I had an active social life at home.

Dangerous

Yes, traveling is dangerous. But so is home. When I was in Nicaragua, a story was doing the rounds on Facebook about someone being attacked or threatened by a machete. That very same day, another Facebook story told of a machete attack back in my home city. Which one was scarier? Our anxiety heightens in unfamiliar territory. It's normal. As a survival technique, we are wired to continually be looking for threats. This is a big issue, particularly for women. That's why there's a whole topic on this later. But my experience is, it's only dangerous until you get there. So please, don't let your fears hold you back. It's normal.

Health

I heard a story about a woman who was shocked to wake up with a great big abscess growing on the side of her neck. Or the person who within days suddenly became so ill he was bedridden for weeks. Or worse still... we could go on. We can focus on what could go wrong and never leave our home. Or instead, we could focus on what if nothing went wrong and what an experience we could have.

You may have a health issue that limits you. We're not 18 anymore, so we all share some limitations in terms of our endurance. But there are so many inspiring people who have worked hard on overcoming their physical limitations. It comes down to what we really want and managing what we've got. Of course, things can and will go wrong. It is wise to expect it and have contingency plans for how to deal with any problems. It's like car or house insurance. We are prepared for the worst, but we don't spend every day worrying about what disaster could happen. So, make sure you have good travel insurance – don't leave home without it.

It's also wise to keep your travel insurance and other documents in an online sharable folder (see Resources). Make sure your travel partner or trusted friend or relative has access to the folder as well, keeping them aware of your travel itinerary. As an emergency precaution, when traveling solo, I also kept an online document updated with the contact details of each place I stayed.

With these precautions in place, the next thing is to get out there and live the experience!

THE YOUTHFUL MIDLIFE TRAVELLER

Summary

There are often more reasons to suggest we can't do things we'd like to do, such as travel. But if we investigate each reason, we'll often find it's a myth that can be busted by simply looking at the obstacle from a different perspective.

Chapter 4.
Fears

You've had this yearning to travel the world. You want to feel empowered and confident to take that all-important first step, and then the next step... But beware. Someone will be trying to hold you back. And that someone will most likely be you.

We are often our own worst enemy.

That Voice in Our Head

Every time you get serious about your crazy dream, you can be sure that the voice inside your head will be at the ready to keep you safe and comfortable. That's its job, and it does it well. That's why we need to talk with it.

Some people describe addressing our fears like peeling back each layer of an onion. Each layer may have us shed a tear as we listen to the concerns our inner voice wants to tell us. Each layer will show us reasons why we should stay as we are, to stay safe, familiar, and comfortable. But as we peel back each layer, listen to what it is saying. Don't ignore the chatter; it is simply trying to keep us safe. Answer the "What if" concerns, then peel back the next layer and keep peeling back until you feel you can take action.

And deep down, beyond all the noisy chatter in our heads, we will often find another inner dialogue to listen to - the pull of our heart. It's probably been trying to speak to us over many years. And over the years, we have added layer after layer of reasons not to go. So why not start peeling and allow the pull of your heart to take you to amazing places you never thought possible.

A Hundred reasons
When I came up with my crazy idea of my senior gap year, I discovered what seemed like a hundred reasons not to go. I was too old, what, going for twelve months, on my own...? In the end, I wasn't quite as kind as you may be to the voice inside my head. After many months of listening to my fears, it's

as if I turned to my voice inside my head and finally said, "enough, get over it, we're going." If I hadn't, I would have missed out on amazing life-changing experiences. And by the way, the voice inside the head and I got on really fine after that!

Gary Westfal, author of "Fear is a Thief," says, *"First, you must acknowledge the fear. You have to recognize that you have this fundamental fear of x, whatever it is. Let's say I have a fundamental fear of traveling. You have to get to the core of why you feel that way. Once you have acknowledged the fact that, yes, I am generally fearful or I have anxieties about travel, what is it about the travel that is fearful to you? So, one is admission; two is to confront it, and by confronting it, we break it down"* (Hear Gary Westfal talk about fear in Resources).

Share Ideas Carefully

You may have another challenge - your family and friends. They care for you just like that voice inside your head. Except there's one difference. They can't see the vision your heart is pulling you to. Choose to share your vision and ideas with people who understand you and your dreams. They will help to build your plans and, importantly, your confidence.

THE YOUTHFUL MIDLIFE TRAVELLER

The "yes, you can do this."

Once you are committed and confident, you will be more resilient to the well-intentioned advice from those closest and dearest to you. Stick to your guns. You will not only have the amazing feeling of fulfillment in achieving your dream, but you will become an inspiration to those who naturally cautioned you against your "crazy" idea.

Expect The Worst
Be prepared that things will go wrong. It happens. But remember, what if it doesn't happen, and think about what you could have missed out on if you didn't do it or go. Be open to when it does go wrong. There are not too many problems that don't have a solution. The dilemma is we don't often see them. Be open, and you will inevitably work through it. It's the power of human nature we all have. Plus, it's when things go wrong that make the best story. Make sure your story is a great one, so look forward to the hiccups along the way.

Jo Principle
I once asked my sister, who was a flight attendant at

the time, how she managed to remain so positive. When everyone else would get angry at little annoyances, she always seemed to remain positive. Her secret principle, she told me, is to expect the worst and get on with it. When it doesn't happen or isn't as bad as you expect, it's like getting a huge reward. An example she explained, was by expecting a short flight to be well over half an hour late, while people were openly frustrated if it was just 10 minutes late, she was excited it was nowhere near as bad as she had allowed! So be prepared for the worst so you can be excited for most times it doesn't happen.

Summary
Feeling empowered is not just about following your heart and your dreams, but also about listening to each fear. Remembering that our fear's job is to keep us safe. But to nurture our dreams into reality, we need to peel each fear back, understand it and when appropriate, let it go. Then let your adventure come to life, being prepared for the challenges... and the many rewards.

THE YOUTHFUL MIDLIFE TRAVELLER

Chapter 5
Your Travel Style Summary

In this section, we embarked on a journey to gain clarity about the type of travel experience you are seeking and to identify any obstacles that may be holding you back.

We explored the diverse spectrum of travel experiences, ranging from luxury to pure adventure, and we delved into the advantages of traveling like a local. We highlighted the merits of independent travel, including the cultural enrichment and mental health benefits it offers. Additionally, we considered different forms of travel, such as package tours and a blend of independent and guided tours. We encouraged you to reflect on where you want to be and where you currently stand, often advising that taking baby steps can be a wise approach.

We discussed the duration of travel and introduced the concept of living like a local. Furthermore, we examined the purposes of your travel, emphasizing the importance of defining your aims or staying open to discovering new ones. We addressed various myths that can deter people from traveling and endeavoured to dispel them. Finally, we explored the fears that may be concealing your true desires.

To gain a clear understanding of your preferred travel style, let's reverse-engineer the process:

1. Decide what your heart is compelling you to do.
2. Find the factors that are inhibiting you from acting.
3. Consider your travel purpose—whether it's well-defined or open to exploration.
4. Specify the type of travel experience you envision, along with the level of independence you want.
5. Evaluate your current confidence and knowledge levels.
6. Use the rest of this guide to establish the necessary steps to reach your travel goals.
7. Address your fears individually, peeling back each

layer to work through them.

I recommend dedicating some time to each of these points, even if you don't have complete clarity on all of them initially. As you progress through the guide, you can expect that these points will become clearer. If, upon revisiting them, some elements stay unclear, don't hesitate to make an educated guess. Taking action is more valuable than not taking action at all. Even in the worst-case scenario where things don't go as planned, it's better to have tried and failed than to have never tried at all. However, it's unlikely to come to that. Travel, like life, is a series of decisions. Each day, you'll face choices about which path to take, what to do, or where to go. You may never know the outcome of the alternatives, but what you can control is making the choice you do make an incredible and fulfilling experience. This way, you can journey without regrets.

PLANNING YOUR ADVENTURE

Chapter 6
Choosing Your Destination

Selecting your travel destination is a pivotal decision that can greatly influence your overall experience. To make an informed choice, you should engage in research, which can be as simple as conversing with experienced travellers, consulting travel books, and using online resources.

Consider your interests—whether it's architecture, history, food, art, nature, hiking, or cultural immersion. It's important to contemplate your budget and the destination's currency exchange rate, as these factors significantly impact travel costs. For instance, most European countries are more expensive compared to many Latin American or Asian destinations.

Seasons play a crucial role in your travel plans, particularly for outdoor activities like skiing and hiking. Traveling during peak tourist seasons can lead to higher costs and need advanced booking for accommodations. Avoiding peak seasons, such as opting for shoulder or off-peak times, often offers more flexibility in terms of accommodation choices and better prices. However, be prepared for potential weather inconveniences in off-peak seasons.

In destinations where peak tourist season and off-peak seasons vary, it's possible to experience limited access to services when traveling outside the main season. Flexibility and an adventurous spirit can help overcome such challenges.

Traveling during peak tourist seasons has its merits as well, with bustling activities, favourable weather conditions, and special events and festivals to enjoy. If these elements align with your travel desires, then planning your trip around these times can be a delightful experience.

Destination costs should be evaluated in conjunction with your budget and travel duration. Low-cost destinations can allow for extended travel, aligning your expenses with your typical living costs at home. Regions like Latin America, Spain, Eastern Europe, or Southeast Asia offer cost-effective travel experiences, including affordable accommodation options such as hotels, guest houses, hostels, and Airbnb. Various websites provide detailed cost breakdowns by country, offering insights into suitable destinations for your budget (see Resources).

It's advisable to consult government travel advice, although it should be considered with some discretion. High-level travel warnings may apply to specific regions within a country, while most other areas still are unaffected and accessible to travellers. Online forums and Facebook groups tailored to expats in your preferred destination can provide valuable insights and firsthand information about local conditions and challenges.

Your level of language ability should also be factored into your destination choice, especially for extended stays. Opting for a destination where a sizable expatriate community speaks your native language can provide a social foundation to connect with and access the local culture. Connecting with expats offers insights beyond typical tours, providing opportunities for longer-term "live like a local" experiences.

In summary, when choosing your destination:
• Consider low-cost destinations to prolong your travel and enhance cultural experiences.
• Evaluate the seasons for accommodations and costs, factoring in the availability of travel activities.
• Use online tools to assess the costs associated with various countries.
• Check government travel advice but interpret it wisely.
• Seek destinations with expat communities to establish social connections and embrace local living experiences.

Chapter 7
Research Destinations

Before embarking on your journey, you have the option to conduct thorough research on various aspects of your destination, such as its culture, history, architecture, food, or art. Delving into these topics can provide you with a deeper understanding of the destination you are about to explore and assist in determining where you want to travel. However, some travellers, like me, prefer to defer extensive research until they arrive at their destination. Upon arriving in a new region, I often rely on web resources, guidebooks, and advice from fellow travellers and local accommodation staff to discover key features and must-see attractions.

Several information-rich resources are available to help you in planning the specifics of your trip. Google, Lonely Planet, and TripAdvisor are valuable platforms where you can find detailed information on various destinations. Lonely Planet offers comprehensive information on specific locations, making its guides a useful companion during your travels. Additionally, you can explore travel companies' itineraries to find the highlights of a destination.

While printed guidebooks have their merits, I recommend using electronic versions. They may not provide the tactile experience of flipping through physical pages, but they offer the advantage of portability and eliminate the added bulk and weight of physical books in your luggage. Moreover, carrying a guidebook can make you appear more like a tourist and potentially vulnerable as a target of ill intent, compared to using a digital guide on your smartphone.

Summary
Researching destinations is a crucial step in your travel planning process. You can choose to delve deeply into the culture, history, and attractions of your chosen places before your trip or gather information as you go. Online resources and electronic guidebooks are excellent tools to enhance

your travel experience and navigate your chosen destinations effectively.

THE YOUTHFUL MIDLIFE TRAVELLER

Chapter 8
Getting There

Flights and Flight Apps

When it comes to booking your flights, there are various websites and apps that can help you find great deals and create your travel itinerary (see Resources). These resources are particularly useful if you want to remain flexible with your travel dates, as they can display the cheapest days to fly. In some cases, you might discover excellent deals by scanning flight prices for an entire month. Keep in mind that while international return flights can sometimes be cheaper than one-way options, breaking your journey into segments and searching for each leg individually can lead to cost savings.

For those who are feeling adventurous and open to exploring new places, certain apps offer an "Anywhere" option for destination (See Resources).

You can select your departure city, choose a date range, and the app will display prices for various destinations. This feature can help you find the most affordable destination based on your preferences.

Consider exploring around-the-world fares, which are often a cost-effective way to visit multiple destinations during an extensive journey. Keep in mind that flight costs are influenced by the time of year, so booking well in advance can save you money. Typically, prices are lower when booked further from your departure date.

Flying Using Frequent Flyer Points
Believe it or not, an around-the-world ticket for under $300 USD is possible. It may sound too good to be true, but it's a legitimate option. For example, Qantas, part of the Oneworld alliance, offers an around-the-world ticket that can be bought using frequent flyer points. These tickets come with certain restrictions, such as traveling in one direction and completing your journey within a year. While planning and booking such a trip can be time-consuming, the savings make it well worth the effort. When building your itinerary, you have flexibility

about the number of miles travelled, the number of connections, and the choice for stopovers in up to five cities.

Some typical requirements include booking your trip at least 8 days before departure, completing your journey across at least three continents, and having an itinerary with fewer than 16 total segments. Remember that you must travel in one continuous direction around the globe.

For more information and general tips on creating a Oneworld Explorer itinerary, please refer to Resources.

Credit Card Sign-Ups
If you don't have enough frequent flyer points for your around-the-world ticket, don't worry. You can accumulate the necessary points quickly and easily. Several banks offer sign-up bonuses for their credit cards, and all you typically need to do is spend a specified amount within the first few months to earn a substantial number of points. These points can be used for your airfare. Keep in mind that most credit cards with such bonuses come with an annual fee,

usually in the range of three to four hundred dollars. Make sure to assess whether the benefit of accumulating frequent flyer points this way outweigh the annual fee. After testing multiple cards, you can decide which one to keep, a topic I'll discuss later. It's important to note this method is best suited for individuals who pay off their credit card balances in full each month.

Repositioning Cruises

For those with time flexibility, repositioning cruises offer a luxurious and cost-effective way to travel. These cruises occur at the end of each cruise season when liners are relocated to a different part of the world for the next season's launch. One-way repositioning cruises are typically offered at discounted prices, making them a fantastic option to explore new destinations. They can take you to places you might not have considered and are another exciting way to begin or extend your adventure. Additionally, some repositioning cruises do not charge a supplement for single travellers, making them highly affordable for solo adventurers. These cruises often supply similar entertainment, meal options, and services to regular cruises.

See Resources for more information.

Summary:
- Flight apps simplify the process of planning your itinerary.
- Frequent flyer points can provide a cost-effective way to book your flights.
- Credit card sign-up bonuses are an excellent means of accumulating frequent flyer points.
- Repositioning cruises offer an exciting choice for those without time constraints.

Chapter 9
Getting Around

In most countries, flying is a convenient option for traveling long distances. It offers speed and efficiency, but it also comes with some disadvantages. You must consider the travel time and cost to get to the airport, as well as the extra time needed for check-in and security procedures, both at your departure and arrival locations. In contrast, land transport, such as trains and buses, can offer more relaxed, immersive, and cost-effective ways to travel. Here's a closer look at various modes of transportation:

Trains:
Traveling by train is a great way to experience a country up close and personal. It allows you to interact with locals and see the landscape as you pass through it. Trains offer more room to move around and provide opportunities for dining. A sleeper car

can further enhance your journey. Keep in mind that buying advance tickets can in some destinations save you up to 30% on your travel expenses.

Buses:
Buses can be an excellent choice for long and short trips within a continent, even in economically challenged countries. Long-distance bus networks in regions like Central and South America and Southeast Asia are often of high quality and comfort. These networks feature a variety of options, from local open-air pickup trucks to luxury coach lines with full-length beds. Although the bus system may appear chaotic, it is efficient. When language barriers arise, seeking local advice and cross-referencing information with multiple sources can help ensure you're on the right track.

Tourist Bus/Train vs. Local Equivalent:
In many places, a premium bus or train network operates for tourists alongside a cheaper public or local network. Opting for the local version can provide a more authentic experience at an equally comfortable level.

Booking Ahead or Last Minute:
In peak seasons, especially in popular destinations, booking flights, trains, or intercity buses months in advance may be cost-effective. However, this approach limits flexibility. Weigh the convenience of last-minute bookings against the higher cost and decide which parts of your itinerary to book in advance.

Car Hire:
Rental cars are a practical choice for travel within a continent, depending on factors such as time, distance, flexibility, and cost. Renting a car offers greater freedom but can also introduce stress and fatigue, particularly for solo travellers. The cost-effectiveness of car hire varies, but it is generally more advantageous for groups.

Ride Share and Taxi:
When arriving in a new city or at an airport, using ride-sharing services like Uber is a preferred choice for safety and cost transparency. These app-based services eliminate the risk of fare negotiation or currency issues. Ensure you have internet access

upon arriving in a new country to use a ride-sharing app or to check taxi fares. Most airports offer free Wi-Fi access, but once you leave the terminal, you'll need mobile data for internet access.

Bicycles:
For local travel within a city, ride-sharing bicycles or buying a second-hand bike can be a great option. Many cities have bike-sharing programs, and buying a second-hand bike offers flexibility for longer stays. Biking can also be an enjoyable way to explore a city or travel between towns on dedicated bike paths.

Motor Bikes:
In Asian countries, riding a motorbike or scooter is an exciting way to experience local life and traffic. Make sure your travel insurance covers motorbike use and consider the fine print to understand the limitations. If you're planning a longer motorbike trip, you can find resources online from travellers who have done similar journeys.

Walking:
Walking is the most fundamental form of human transport and offers a close up look at your

destination. It allows you to experience local life and feel the pulse of the place you're visiting. Staying in the heart of a city and walking as much as possible, supplemented with local public transport, is a strategy many experienced travellers adopt. Walking tours are also an excellent way to get acquainted with a new city, and many are available for free, funded by donations.

Summary:
- Flying is efficient if you have limited time and need to travel long distances between countries.
- Trains are an excellent way to experience a country, offering a more immersive and cost-effective mode of travel.
- Buses can be a relaxing way to travel within a continent, even in economically challenged countries.
- Car hire is a choice but may introduce stress and is generally more suitable for groups.
- Ride-sharing services and taxis are preferred choices for local transport within a city.
- Bicycles are great for exploring cities or dedicated bike paths.
- Motorbikes offer an exciting way to experience local traffic, especially in Asian countries.
- Walking allows you to get a close feel for your

THE YOUTHFUL MIDLIFE TRAVELLER

destination and is often favoured by experienced travellers.

See Resources for more information.

Chapter 10
Accommodation

When it comes to booking accommodation, there are various approaches you can take depending on your travel style and preferences. Here are some considerations for booking accommodation while travelling:

Booking on the Fly or in Advance:
Whether you choose to book your accommodation in advance or on the go depends on your travel style and the destination. Booking in advance provides the security of knowing where you'll stay and can be a better option during peak tourist seasons or for shorter vacations. However, booking on the fly allows for greater flexibility, as you can decide where to stay once you arrive at your destination.

Accommodation Booking Apps:

Accommodation booking apps like Airbnb, Booking.com, and others offer a wide range of options, from luxury hotels to budget hostels and everything in between. These apps typically provide photos, ratings, and written reviews, making it easier to choose a place that suits your preferences and budget. Setting search filters for ratings and price ranges can help narrow down your options.

Budget-Level Accommodation:

Staying in budget-level accommodations like hostels, guesthouses, bed and breakfasts, or even huts on the beach can provide more authentic travel experiences. If the basic facilities, such as the bed and bathroom, are clean, you can find excellent options. Many hostels offer private rooms for those who prefer a bit more privacy.

Alternative Accommodation Options:

- **Hostels**: Many hostels are professionally run and supply a social hub. You can choose between more vibrant party hostels and quieter ones.
- **Short-Term Apartments**: Websites like Airbnb offer a wide range of options, from shared rooms to

entire apartments. Homestays and couch-surfing can also be affordable choices.

- **Lodgings in Exchange for Time:** Consider opportunities to exchange your time for board and lodgings. Various services list organizations that offer such exchanges, giving you a chance to connect with local people.

- **House Sitting:** House sitting is a choice for longer stays, and it typically involves looking after a house and pets. You can register as a house sitter on specialized websites or join related Facebook groups.

- **Home Swap:** Home exchange allows you to swap homes with someone in another destination. While it requires trust and advanced arrangements, it can be a cost-effective way to experience living like a local.

Choosing the Right Accommodation:
When selecting accommodation, keep in mind your travel style, preferences, and priorities. Consider factors such as location, price, amenities, and reviews. Be prepared to read between the lines in reviews to ensure you are making an informed choice.

Accommodation for Longer Stays:

If you plan to stay in a destination for an extended period, consider that accommodation costs can be significantly discounted for longer bookings, including Airbnb. Living like a local can be both more affordable and rewarding.

Safety and Backup:

Always pick up a business card of your accommodation or make a note of the name and address. Having this information on hand is essential in case you get lost or need to communicate with a taxi driver, especially when your phone's battery is low.

Summary

Your choice of accommodation can greatly impact your travel experience. Whether you book in advance or on the fly, opt for budget-level accommodations or explore alternative options, there's a wealth of choices to suit your preferences and budget. Keep safety in mind and make the most of the opportunities to connect with local people and immerse yourself in the culture of your destination.

See Resources for more information including a list of useful apps to source accommodation.

THE YOUTHFUL MIDLIFE TRAVELLER

Chapter 11
Travel Insurance

Travel insurance is a vital aspect of trip planning. It provides financial protection and peace of mind when you're exploring the world. Here are some key considerations for securing travel insurance:

The Necessity of Travel Insurance:
The cardinal rule of travel is if you can't afford travel insurance, then you shouldn't travel. The cost of a travel mishap or emergency can be far more significant than the expense of insurance.

Health Insurance Benefits:
Depending on your country of residence, your health insurance may offer some coverage while you're abroad. In Australia, for example, health insurance companies often suspend premium

payments when policyholders are away for an extended period. This can create cost savings that can be allocated to your travel insurance, essentially providing free coverage. However, it's essential to reinstate your health insurance just before returning home. Be sure to check with your health insurer about the specifics of your coverage.

Variations in Travel Insurance Policies:
Not all travel insurance policies are the same. While they may seem similar at first glance, they often have different terms, conditions, and coverage. Reading the fine print is crucial because how one policy defines a particular benefit may differ significantly from another. While insurance may not seem important until you need to make a claim, the time spent researching policies will pay off in case of an incident. Pay attention to any conditions related to specific activities you plan to undertake during your trip, such as skiing, water sports, or motorbike rental.

Customized Coverage:
When selecting a travel insurance policy, look for one that aligns with your unique travel needs. Consider your destination, the duration of your trip,

the activities you plan to engage in, and any pre-existing medical conditions. This allows you to tailor your coverage to suit your requirements.

Payment Flexibility:
Some insurance providers offer flexibility in their payment arrangements. For instance, you may be able to purchase coverage for specific periods, such as the first few months of your trip. You can then extend the coverage without incurring added costs as long as you keep making payments.

World Nomads:
World Nomads is a well-known travel insurance provider that offers coverage for travellers. What sets it apart is the ability to buy insurance both from home and while on the road. You can also make claims online from anywhere in the world. While World Nomads is popular, it's essential to research various insurance providers to find the best one for your needs.

Online Research:
To choose the right travel insurance, conduct internet research to find options that align with your

requirements. Begin by making a list of your specific needs and preferences. With this list in hand, you can begin your search for an insurance policy that matches your criteria.

Summary

Travel insurance is a fundamental part of your trip planning process. It provides financial security and ensures you are prepared for unforeseen circumstances. While it might not be the most exciting part of trip planning, the time spent researching and selecting the right policy will prove valuable should you ever need to make a claim. Make sure your insurance aligns with your travel plans, offers flexibility in payment, and covers all the activities and destinations you plan to explore.

See Resources for more information.

Chapter 12
Visas

Understanding visa requirements is a crucial aspect of international travel. Depending on your nationality and the countries you plan to visit, the need for visas can vary. Here are some key considerations when dealing with visas:

1. Visa Requirements:
The need for visas depends on your nationality and the countries you intend to visit. Researching visa requirements is a crucial step in trip planning. Many countries have their own visa regulations, and it's your responsibility to ensure you meet them. You'll typically need to prearrange a visa for entry into some countries.

2. Researching Visa Requirements:
When you research visa requirements, you'll also

want to consider the length of stay permitted in each country you plan to visit. Different countries have different policies about how long tourists are allowed to stay. The duration may vary depending on your nationality as well.

3. Prearranged Visas:

For some countries, especially those with stricter visa regulations, you may need to apply for a visa well in advance of your planned travel. This process often requires supplying various documents, passport-sized photos, and sometimes an interview at the embassy or consulate.

4. Visa Application Timing:

Visa applications can take time, and processing periods may vary. It's advisable to start the application process at least a few weeks, or even months, before your intended travel date to avoid any last-minute complications.

5. Special Visa Categories:

If you plan to stay in a foreign country for an extended period or want to work or retire there, you may need to explore specific visa categories, such as retirement visas or working visas. Some countries offer retirement visas that require you to prove a certain level of financial support.

6. Visa Costs:

Be aware that obtaining a visa often involves fees, and the amount can differ significantly between countries. These costs are typically non-refundable, so it's essential to carefully review the requirements and fees before submitting your application.

7. Entry Payments:

In addition to visa fees, some countries may require an entry payment or fee upon arrival. This fee is typically payable in cash and often in US dollars. It's advisable to carry some cash with you when traveling to cover these expenses.

8. Online Resources:

To research visa requirements for specific countries, you can perform a simple Google search, such as "visa requirements for [country name]." Many online resources and government websites supply detailed information about visa requirements and processes.

THE YOUTHFUL MIDLIFE TRAVELLER

Summary

Understanding visa requirements is essential for international travel. Visa regulations can vary widely between countries, so it's essential to research the specific requirements for the countries you plan to visit well in advance. Take note of application timelines, fees, and any other requirements to ensure a smooth and hassle-free travel experience.

See also Resources.

Chapter 13
Health & Immunisations

Ensuring your health and well-being during your travels is of utmost importance. Here are some key considerations about health and immunizations:

1. Consultation with Your Doctor:

It's recommended to consult with your GP (General Practitioner) or family doctor at least six to eight weeks before your departure. This visit serves two essential purposes: a general medical check-up and advice on health preparations for your specific travel destinations.

2. Prescription Medications:

If you're on prescription medications, discuss your travel plans with your doctor. Ensure you have an adequate supply for the duration of your trip and consider asking for a written prescription in case you need a refill during your travels. Additionally, you should carry your medications in their original labelled containers.

3. Vaccinations:
Research the recommended and needed vaccinations for the countries you plan to visit. Depending on your destination, you may need specific immunizations to protect against diseases such as yellow fever, typhoid, hepatitis, or malaria. Some countries may even need proof of certain vaccinations for entry.

4. Dental Care:
Consider visiting your dentist well before your departure for a dental check-up. Dental work can be expensive abroad, so it's a good idea to address any potential issues before you leave.

5. Medical Records:
Keep an updated record of your vaccinations and medical history. This can be valuable in case you need medical attention while abroad and can help healthcare providers make informed decisions about

your care.

6. Fitness and Health:

Being reasonably fit and active can be an asset during your travels, especially if you plan to engage in physically demanding activities. Regular exercise and maintaining good health can enhance your overall travel experience.

7. First Aid Kit:

Pack a small medical first aid kit. Essential items include band-aids, bandages, anti-diarrheal medication, sunburn cream, malaria pills if needed, insect repellent, and other basic medical supplies. Additionally, items like duct tape and pawpaw cream can be versatile and useful.

8. Food and Water Safety:

Be cautious with food and water consumption, particularly in countries with different food hygiene standards. To minimize the risk of food-related illnesses:
- Choose bottled water, ensuring the cap is sealed.
- Use carbonated water as it is more challenging to counterfeit.

- Avoid ice and food that has been peeled or sliced.
- Prefer freshly prepared, piping hot food over hotel buffets.
- Spicy foods are not a guarantee of safety but can add flavour.

9. Traveller's Diarrhea:
Traveller's diarrhea, often referred to as "Bali Belly" in certain regions, can be a common concern. Be cautious with what you eat and drink and keep an over-the-counter medication for diarrhea in your first aid kit.

10. Personal Hygiene:
Practicing good personal hygiene, such as frequent handwashing, is essential to prevent illness while traveling. Carry hand sanitizer for use when clean water and soap are unavailable.

Summary
Your health and well-being are crucial aspects of your travel preparations. Consult with your doctor, get the recommended vaccinations, keep a basic medical first aid kit, and be cautious with your food and water choices to ensure a safe and enjoyable

travel experience. Your health and safety should be a top priority during your adventures.

THE YOUTHFUL MIDLIFE TRAVELLER

Chapter 14
Documents & Checklist

Organizing and managing your travel documents is essential for a smooth and stress-free travel experience. Here are some important considerations and recommendations:

1. Digital Document Storage:
To ensure easy access to your travel documents, use cloud storage services like Google Drive, Dropbox, or OneDrive. You can create dedicated folders for different categories, such as travel insurance, itineraries, vaccination records, and identification documents.

2. Smartphone Management:
Use your smartphone to store digital copies of essential travel documents. Create a dedicated folder

or use a secure document management app for this purpose. Make sure your phone is protected with a strong PIN or password and enable fingerprint or facial recognition if available.

3. Paper Copies:
While digital documents are convenient, it's a good practice to have paper copies of critical documents, such as your passport, driver's license, and visa if required. Store these paper copies separately from the originals.

4. Trusted Contacts:
Ensure that a trusted friend or family member knows how to access your cloud storage or smartphone documents in case of emergencies. Provide them with the necessary access details or share specific folders with them.

5. Travel Insurance:
Keep a digital and paper copy of your travel insurance policy. Make sure it includes details on coverage, emergency contact numbers, and any exclusions or limitations.

6. Passport and Visa:
Ensure your passport has at least six months of validity beyond your planned return date. If you need a visa for your destination, have digital and paper copies of the visa and any related documentation.

7. Travel Itinerary:
Organize your travel itinerary, including flight details, accommodation reservations, and contact information, in a dedicated folder or app. Having this readily accessible can help with last-minute changes and reference during your journey.

8. Vaccination Records:
If your travel requires specific vaccinations, keep a record of these and ensure they are up to date. Digital copies in your travel documents folder are ideal.

9. Checklist:
Create a checklist of items you need to take care of before and during your trip. Include tasks like packing, securing your home, booking transportation, and more. A checklist helps you stay organized and ensures that nothing important is

overlooked. You can find templates for travel checklists in Resources.

10. Regular Updates:
Periodically review and update your travel documents and checklist as needed. Ensure your passport, travel insurance, and vaccinations remain current.

Traveling with well-organized documents and a checklist can significantly reduce stress during your trip and help you quickly address any unexpected situations. It's a critical part of travel preparation that contributes to a more enjoyable and hassle-free adventure.

Chapter 15
Planning Your Adventure Summary

Planning your adventure is a crucial step in ensuring a successful and enjoyable trip. Here's a summary of the key points covered in this section:

1. Destination and Season:
Choose your destination carefully, considering factors like the season, travel warnings, and language barriers. Research is essential to make informed decisions.

2. Flight Savings:
Look for ways to save on flights, such as using frequent flyer points, travel credit cards, or considering repositioning cruises as cost-effective alternatives.

3. Overland Travel:
If time allows, consider overland travel options like

buses, trains, or rental vehicles to experience the country more intimately and connect with locals.

4. Accommodation:

Use booking apps to conveniently find a range of accommodations, from luxury hotels to budget hostels. For longer stays, explore options like house sitting, house swapping, or lodging in exchange for time to save on costs.

5. Travel Insurance:

Travel insurance is a must to cover potential misadventures. Compare policies to ensure they meet your specific needs and provide necessary coverage.

6. Visas:

Check the visa requirements for your destination and make necessary arrangements well in advance. Be prepared to pay any entry fees in cash, often in US dollars or local currency.

7. Health and Food:

Consult your doctor for medical check-ups, vaccinations, and advice on prescription medicines. Be cautious with food and water in unfamiliar places and follow general guidelines to reduce the risk of illness.

8. Document Management:
Organize your travel documents, including digital and paper copies, and store them securely. Create a checklist to stay organized before and during your trip.

9. Gratitude:
Show appreciation to your stomach for its resilience when trying new and exotic cuisines.

10. Plan Your Basics:
Start your planning with essential details like your destination and transportation. Equip yourself with relevant apps and documentation to make informed decisions on the go.

By following these guidelines and staying organized, you can embark on your adventure with confidence, making the most of your travel experience while staying safe and cost-effective. Happy travels!

THE YOUTHFUL MIDLIFE TRAVELLER

TRAVEL SMARTS

Chapter 16
Solo Travelling

Solo traveling can be an incredibly rewarding experience, offering independence, personal growth, and the chance to truly immerse yourself in your journey. Here's a summary of what to consider when traveling alone:

Traveling with a Partner:
- Traveling with a friend or partner provides companionship and shared experiences.
- It's an opportunity to create lasting memories together and support each other during the journey.

Solo Travel:

- Traveling alone may be your only choice or your preferred choice.
- Solo travel can be daunting at first, but it offers a unique sense of freedom and personal growth.
- Overcome any self-consciousness such as dining alone and embrace the opportunity for self-discovery.

Considerations for Solo Travellers:

- Be aware of your feelings about potential perceptions of others when dining alone or visiting certain destinations.
- Women may face different challenges and safety concerns, but many women enjoy solo travel with precautions. (See Resources where women solo travellers share their experiences).
- Adapt your accommodation choices to your social needs, opting for hostels, local stays, or hotels accordingly.
- Embrace solo travel's social nature; it often leads to meeting more people.

Technology for Connection:
- Smartphones and technology make staying connected with loved ones easy.
- Use social media, video calls, and blogs (See Resources) to share your journey with friends and family.
- Leverage technology to create and maintain connections with fellow travellers and locals.

Solo travel can offer profound personal experiences, allowing you to explore the world at your own pace. Whether you're traveling alone by choice or necessity, embrace the freedom and growth it brings, and use technology to stay connected and share your journey with others.

THE YOUTHFUL MIDLIFE TRAVELLER

Chapter 17
Earning an Income While Travelling

Earning an income while traveling can help you maintain a sense of balance, ward off travel burnout, and even offset some of your travel expenses. Here are some key points to consider:

Small Business:
- Running an online business allows you to work from anywhere with an internet connection.
- While it might feel like you're always connected to work, this compromise can make long-term travel with less travel burnout and more economically viable.

Skills:
- Consider your specialized knowledge-based skills;

there's a global market for your expertise.
- Explore freelance working sites to find opportunities that match your skills.
- If your job or business can be done remotely, discuss the possibility of working while traveling with your partners or boss.

Teaching English:
- Teaching English is a popular choice with high demand worldwide.
- In some countries, you can teach without formal qualifications, but it's wise to investigate obtaining English teaching certifications.
- Teaching English online is another flexible way that allows you to be your own boss, set your hours, and work from anywhere.

See Resources for more information.

If earning an income while traveling interests you, research the visa requirements for your intended countries and any work restrictions. Explore the possibilities, as there are various ways to support your travels and maintain financial stability while on the road.

While not income earning, volunteering or learning new skills can also enhance your travel experience and provide balance.

THE YOUTHFUL MIDLIFE TRAVELLER

Chapter 18
Travelling Longer Is Cheaper

Traveling for an extended period offers unique opportunities for significant cost savings. By choosing the right destination and season, along with effective planning, you can potentially live abroad for less than the cost of living at home. Here are some ways to make this possible:

Accommodation:
- Consider staying in one location for an extended period, as this often allows for better accommodation deals, including short-term rentals through real estate agents or homestays.
- Airbnb typically offers discounts for extended homestays, making it a cost-effective choice.

Home Cost:
- If you own property, you can rent it out while you're away, which can help cover at least your travel accommodation expenses.
- For renters, you can end your lease agreement and redirect what you'd normally spend on rent and utilities toward your travel budget.
- Consider minimizing clutter and potentially selling furniture before your trip to reduce storage costs.

Car:
- If you own a car, selling it before your trip can help you avoid ongoing expenses like registration, insurance, and depreciation.
- You'll find that cars are readily available when you return.

By managing your accommodation, offsetting home and car costs, and potentially earning an income while traveling, an extended trip can be an economical way to experience the world. With careful planning, you can turn your travel dreams into a reality while saving money compared to staying at home.

Chapter 19
Travel Smarts Summary

This chapter sums up some key travel smarts to keep in mind:

1. Solo Travel:
If you don't have a travel partner, don't let that stop you from exploring the world. Solo travel can be a fulfilling and enriching experience. Use technology to stay connected with loved ones.

2. Earning an Income:
If you want to extend your travels or balance your budget, consider options for earning money while on the road. You can run an online business, offer your skills as a freelancer, or even teach English online or in person.

3. Traveling Longer:

Consider extending your travel duration, even if you're traveling solo. Look for ways to offset your travel costs, like renting out your home or selling your car. This can allow you to travel at a similar cost to living at home and make your travel dreams come true.

4. Flexible Itineraries:

Stay open to alternative plans. Be willing to stretch your comfort zone and think creatively to satisfy your travel needs. In some cases, taking side trips or finding alternatives to your initial plans can lead to unique and rewarding experiences.

With these travel smarts in mind, you're well-prepared to embark on your journey with confidence and the potential for a life-changing adventure.

TRAVEL ESSENTIALS

Chapter 20
What to Pack

Packing smart is a crucial part of successful travel. Here are some key points to consider when deciding what to pack:

1. Travel Light:
Consider traveling with a backpack rather than a suitcase for added mobility and versatility. Backpacks are more suitable for navigating cobblestone streets and uneven terrain, making them a popular choice for many travellers.

2. Quality Over Quantity:

Instead of packing a wide variety of outfits, focus on quality, versatile clothing items that can be mixed and matched. Quick-drying fabrics are useful, as you can wash them in the evening and have them ready to wear the next day.

3. Minimalist Approach:

Don't overpack. When selecting clothing, consider that you can often get by with half of what you initially plan to take. Embrace a minimalist mindset and pack only the essentials.

4. Interchangeable Wardrobe:

Ensure that your clothing items can be easily mixed and matched. This creates the illusion of having more outfit options with fewer pieces.

5. Laundry on the Go:

Prepare to do some laundry during your trip. Most accommodations have facilities, and quick-dry clothing makes it easy. You can wash your clothes in the shower, wring them out, and twist them dry in a towel before hanging to dry.

6. Donate or Mail:

Consider buying items as needed or donating clothing that you no longer need during your travels. Mailing items home can also be a choice if you find yourself with excess belongings.

7. Selecting the Right Luggage:

When choosing your luggage, prioritize lightweight, waterproof, and durable options that will suit your travel needs.

Remember that traveling light makes your journey more manageable and enjoyable. By following these guidelines, you can travel with just the essentials and make the most of your adventure without unnecessary baggage.

For a detailed checklist, check Resources.

THE YOUTHFUL MIDLIFE TRAVELLER

Chapter 21
Cash and Credit Cards

Managing your finances while traveling is essential. Here are some key points to consider about cash and credit cards:

1. Emergency Cash:
Carry a small amount of emergency cash (at least $100) in the local currency of the country you're visiting. This cash can be helpful in situations where you may not have immediate access to ATMs or card payments.

2. Travel Debit Card:
Obtain a travel debit card linked to your savings account. These cards are designed for international use and allow you to make ATM withdrawals and card payments in the local currency of the country you're visiting. Make sure travel card is Visa as a

number of ATMs don't accept Mastercard. Use your banking app to transfer funds from your savings account to your travel debit card when needed.

3. ATM Withdrawals:

Upon arriving in a new country, find the nearest ATM at the airport or within the city to withdraw local currency. Transfer funds to your travel debit card before making withdrawals, ensuring the card balance is kept near zero when not in use.

4. Frequent Flyer Credit Card:

Consider using a frequent flyer credit card for purchases during your travels. This allows you to earn frequent flyer points with every transaction, contributing to future travel opportunities. Check your credit card's banking app to track transactions and verify their accuracy.

5. Currency Exchange:

When leaving a country, use currency exchange booths at airports or bus terminals to convert any remaining local currency back to US dollars or your home currency. The conversion rate may not be as favourable as at a bank, but it's better than holding onto unused currencies.

6. Currency Exchange Apps:

Consider using currency exchange rate apps to check the rates offered at exchange booths and ensure you're getting a fair deal.

7. Password Management Apps:

To keep track of various passwords, especially for financial accounts, use a secure password management app that encrypts and stores your login information. Ensure that the app syncs across your devices for convenience.

By following these tips, you can effectively manage your finances during your travels, ensuring you have access to the necessary funds and that your financial information remains secure.

THE YOUTHFUL MIDLIFE TRAVELLER

Chapter 22
Managing Your Money

Making Your Own ATM Machine:

In some situations, you may find yourself in need of cash without an ATM nearby. One creative solution I used, is to find a restaurant or establishment that accepts credit cards and then exchange cash with other patrons who are paying with a card. This way, you can obtain the cash you need for your daily expenses or emergencies.

Managing Loss of Credit Card and Cash:
Losing your credit card and cash can be a challenging experience, but having a plan can help you navigate this situation effectively. Here are some steps to consider:

- Don't Panic: Stay calm and focus on finding a solution.

- Seek Assistance: If you're traveling with a partner, you have a built-in support system. Traveling solo, however, may require some resourcefulness.

Travel Cards as Pairs:
If you have a backup travel card, hide one in your backpack along with some emergency cash. This way, if you lose your primary wallet and card, you can access the backup card, unblock it using your bank app, and transfer money to continue your journey. The hidden cash can be used for immediate expenses.

Using Western Union:
Western Union is a global service available in many locations. It can be a reliable source of cash when you're in a tight spot. Have a family member or friend deposit money at a Western Union office back home, and they'll provide you with a secret password code. You can then visit a local Western Union office, provide the code, and receive the cash quickly. Be sure to check the commission rate, as it can vary among different locations.

Blocking Your Credit Card:
In the event of a lost or stolen credit card, use your bank app to block the card at once. This will prevent unauthorized use. Notify your bank as soon as possible to report the loss.

Emergency Cash and Credit Card Services:
Visa and Mastercard offer emergency cash services. However, they often use Western Union to issue the funds. You can also request an emergency credit card from Visa, which can be delivered to your location in a few days.

With planning and following these steps, you can effectively manage the loss of your credit card and cash during your travels. It's crucial to have a backup plan and resources in place for such emergencies.

Remember that preparation and quick thinking can make a significant difference when facing unexpected financial challenges while traveling.

THE YOUTHFUL MIDLIFE TRAVELLER

Summary:

Losing access to your money can be a daunting experience, but planning for such situations and having a strategy in place can help you navigate them with confidence. Always have a backup card and cash in a separate location, familiarize yourself with your bank's app, and know how to access emergency cash through resources like Western Union if needed. Preparedness is key when managing your money while on the road. (See also Resources.)

Chapter 23
Technology

Leveraging Technology for Smooth Travel:

Embracing technology during your travels can significantly enhance your experience and make your journey more convenient. Here are some key points to consider:

Getting Familiar with Technology:
Even if you're not tech-savvy, start by familiarizing yourself with the basics of your smartphone and relevant apps for travel. Technology can make your travel more efficient and enjoyable.

Smartphone as Your Travel Command Centre:
Your smartphone is an indispensable tool for independent travel. It serves as your mobile mission

control and aids you in various aspects of your journey, including navigation, communication, and information access.

Internet Connectivity:
Internet access is vital for most aspects of travel, including real-time navigation, restaurant recommendations, translation services, and more. Relying solely on Wi-Fi in hotels and coffee shops may limit your mobility. Downloading maps for offline use can be a smart workaround.

Getting a Local SIM Card:
One of the first things you should do when arriving in a new country is to get a local SIM card with data. This provides you with internet connectivity and allows you to make local calls. Some airports have SIM card providers, but you can often find better deals at local telco shops. Many smartphones offer dual sim card functionality. Consider using one SIM for your international SIM card.

International SIM Cards:
International SIM cards are a choice for travellers who visit multiple countries. These SIM cards

typically offer access in numerous countries with various data rates.

Time Zone Apps:
Using a time zone app can help you keep track of time when crossing multiple time zones. It simplifies the mental arithmetic involved in calculating time differences.

Altimeter Apps:
If you find yourself in areas with varying altitudes, consider using an altimeter app. These apps provide accurate altitude information and can be especially useful if you experience altitude sickness.

Backup Battery:
Always carry a portable mobile phone backup battery. This ensures your phone stays charged even when you're out longer than expected. It's a lifesaver, especially when you rely on your phone for navigation and communication.

Summary
Embracing technology during your travels can significantly enhance your journey's convenience

and efficiency. Utilize your smartphone for various tasks, from navigation to communication. Ensure you have internet access by getting a local SIM card and consider using international SIM cards when visiting multiple countries. Install useful apps to help you in various travel scenarios, and always have a backup battery to keep your phone powered up.

For a list of recommended apps, please refer to Resources for more information.

Chapter 24
Social

Leveraging Social Connections and Smartphone Technology:

During your travels, your smartphone can serve as a powerful tool for staying socially connected, both with loved ones back home and with fellow travellers. Here are some ways to make the most of your smartphone and social apps during your journey:

Easy Communication Through VoIP:
Traditional telco calls are becoming less common while traveling. Voice Over IP (VoIP) apps are an excellent way to make calls back home or locally. These apps work well, provided you have a good internet connection. You can even transfer your landline phone number to a VoIP service, making it appear as though you're calling from home.

Video Calls:

Video calls are a great way to feel connected with family and friends while traveling. Whether you're traveling solo or with a partner, video calls provide a sense of togetherness. Sharing experiences in real time, such as a tour of your current location or an exciting activity, can be particularly memorable.

Social Connection Apps:

Social media apps and platforms can help you stay connected with fellow travellers and meet new people. International social groups and social media communities related to travel are excellent for connecting with like-minded individuals and organizing meetups.

Making Friends and Experiencing Local Life:

Using social media can help you meet people and become part of the local community. Joining language classes allows you to connect with locals and other travellers, fostering a sense of belonging and leading to potential long-lasting friendships.

Facebook Groups and Community Engagement:

Facebook groups and other community forums provide a platform for finding local expatriate communities, sharing experiences, and connecting with fellow travellers. These groups are a valuable resource for advice, recommendations, and meeting people in your destination.

The Value of Volunteering:
Engaging in volunteer opportunities can provide some of the richest travel experiences by connecting you with local people and communities. Volunteering can be a rewarding way to contribute to a local cause and form deep connections with the people you meet.

Overall, you don't have to feel lonely while traveling. Social media apps, VoIP services, and community engagement tools make it easier than ever to connect with loved ones back home and meet new people during your travels. Embracing technology and using social connections can enrich your journey and provide a sense of belonging no matter where you are.

For added resources and recommendations related

to social connections during travel, refer to Resources for more detail.

Chapter 25
Activities

Engaging in Authentic Activities While Traveling:

Travel is about more than just ticking off landmarks and checking destinations off a list. It's about immersing yourself in the local culture, connecting with people, and experiencing authentic activities that provide a deeper understanding of the places you visit. Here are some ways to engage in fulfilling activities while traveling:

Small Group Walking Tours:
Start your exploration of a new city with a small group walking tour. These tours are a great way to get your bearings and learn about the key highlights of a destination. They are also opportunities to meet fellow travellers and locals who share your interest in exploration.

Community Activities:

Going beyond standard tourist experiences, engaging in community activities allows you to interact with locals and contribute to the place you're visiting. Activities such as day hikes, language classes, and volunteering provide opportunities to connect with others and become part of the community.

Language Learning:

Learning the local language, even just the basics, can significantly enhance your travel experience. While language classes may not turn you into a fluent multilingual speaker, they can help you communicate, show respect for the local culture, and form meaningful connections with locals.

Cooking Classes:

Participating in a cooking class is a fun way to learn about local cuisine and culture. These classes often involve hands-on experiences, and you'll likely share your creations with others, fostering a sense of camaraderie.

Cycling and Outdoor Activities:
Joining bike riding groups or engaging in other outdoor activities is a fantastic way to enjoy the natural beauty of a region while socializing with fellow participants. These groups often have a friendly atmosphere and offer opportunities for conversations during breaks.

Creative Classes:
Engaging in creative activities such as painting classes allows you to express your creativity while connecting with others who share similar interests.

Trying New Things:
Travel is the perfect opportunity to step out of your comfort zone and try activities you may not have considered back home. Whether it's surfing, studying architecture, or exploring history on a tour, embrace the youthful spirit of trying new and exciting experiences.

Social Media Apps and Networking:
Leverage social media apps and online communities to find and connect with people who share your interests in various activities (see Resources for apps).

These initial connections can lead to more personal friendships and create lasting memories from your travels.

Summary

Travel is about enriching experiences, and engaging in activities with others can be the key to forming deeper connections, broadening your horizons, and adding meaning to your journey. The activities you choose can balance your travel adventures and provide a sense of fulfillment and purpose. Embrace the opportunity to be youthful and adventurous in your approach to travel, trying new things and forming friendships along the way.

Chapter 26
How to Travel Safely

Is Traveling Dangerous?

Traveling is not inherently more dangerous than staying at home. Accidents and incidents can happen anywhere in the world. It's essential to differentiate between the perception of danger and the actual level of risk. Sometimes, we may feel safer in a foreign destination than in our hometown. Keep in mind that while traveling, you might encounter unfamiliar risks, but many of these can be minimized or avoided through vigilance and informed decision-making.

Overcoming Misconceptions:
Travellers often have misconceptions about the safety of their destinations. News reports, particularly negative ones, can create an exaggerated image of danger. However, just like at home, most

destinations have safe areas and more problematic ones. When you hear about a crisis or disaster abroad, it often affects only a specific region within a country, while the rest stays unaffected.

Heeding Local Advice:
When you travel, pay attention to local advice. Locals and experienced travellers can provide insights into which areas to avoid and how to stay safe. For example, walking tours led by knowledgeable guides can offer valuable information on safety and local customs.

Trust Your Intuition:
Your instincts are your best safety guide. If a situation doesn't feel right, remove yourself from it. Use your common sense and follow your gut feeling when assessing the safety of a place or situation.

Beware of Scams:
Research common scams in your destination by searching online for the city name and the word "scam". Additionally, ask your accommodation provider and other travellers about prevalent scams. Being forewarned can prevent inconvenient and

costly situations.

Carry Identification and Emergency Contacts:
Always carry identification, preferably with an emergency contact number. If you're separated from your travel companions, emergency personnel can use this information to contact someone on your behalf.

Safety for Solo Women Travellers:
Solo female travellers often have specific safety concerns. Several online communities, like "Women Who Travel" and "The Solo Female Traveller Network," cater to female travellers, providing advice, tips, and support.

See Resources where solo women travellers share their travel experience.

Useful Safety Precautions:
Here are some important safety tips:
- Seek local advice from accommodation staff and tourist services.
- Talk to fellow travellers.
- Learn which areas are safe to explore and which to

avoid.
- Stay in well-travelled and well-lit areas.
- Subscribe to government travel advice services.
- Exercise caution on alcohol, drugs, and casual encounters.
- Most importantly, do not let the fear of danger deter you from traveling. The precautions are minimal compared to the immense satisfaction you will gain from experiencing the positive aspects of your journey.

Summary:
Traveling is an adventure, but it's essential to be aware of safety concerns and educate yourself about your destinations. Most safety practices boil down to common sense and vigilance. Don't let fear hold you back; instead, focus on the excitement of exploring the world and remember that the best stories often come from making mistakes and overcoming challenges while traveling.

For a full list of advice tips, see Resources.

Chapter 27
Travel Essentials Summary

Before you embark on your travel adventure, it's essential to prepare the right travel essentials. This section covers various elements to make your journey smoother and more enjoyable.

Travel Light:
One of the secrets to successful travel is packing light. You typically don't need as much as you think, and a backpack is often the best choice for carrying your essentials. Selecting versatile clothing and packing only the essentials can help reduce the weight you carry.

Money Requirements:
Managing your finances is crucial for a stress-free journey. The four primary money requirements for your trip include:

1. A small amount of emergency cash.
2. A Travel Debit Visa card.
3. A regular Visa card.
4. A banking app to manage your finances on the go.

Technology as Your Mission Control:
Your smartphone is a central tool for your travels. It serves as your mission control for staying connected, navigating, and accessing a wide range of travel-related apps. Technology offers many ways to enhance your travel experience, making it more productive and convenient.

Preparing for Emergencies:
It's essential to plan for the worst-case scenario, such as losing your money or important documents. Having a strategy in place to deal with these situations will give you peace of mind while traveling.

Social Connections:
Travel is about people, and your smartphone can help you stay connected with loved ones at home and make new friends on the road. Utilizing various apps and social media platforms can help you keep a sense of belonging and stay in contact with family and

friends.

Engaging in Activities:
Participating in activities is an excellent way to create social connections while providing a sense of balance to your travel. Whether it's joining local tours, cooking classes, language courses, or group hikes, these activities can help you engage with others and enrich your travel experience.

Travel Safety:
Travel does come with risks, but they can be minimized through education and preparation. Understanding the potential dangers in your destination, staying informed about local conditions, and heeding advice from locals, fellow travellers, and government travel advisories are all crucial for ensuring your safety.

Embrace Mistakes and Challenges:
Traveling is an adventure, and sometimes things may not go as planned. Embracing these experiences and viewing them as opportunities to learn and grow can lead to some of your best travel memories and stories to tell. Remember, if you're not making mistakes, you're not trying.

Summary

These essentials provide the foundation for a successful and enjoyable travel experience. By staying organized, informed, and open to new experiences, you can make the most of your journey, embrace the challenges, and come back with a treasure trove of stories.

LIVING LIKE A LOCAL

Chapter 28
Why Live Like a Local

One of the highlights of my senior gap year was spending three months in Spain, particularly in Valencia. While the excitement of backpacking from place to place was undeniable, living like a local offered a unique and special experience. Valencia was chosen as a base due to its vibrant expatriate community, which not only provided a social network but also facilitated a connection to the local community.

Value of a Base:
The idea of using each around-the-world stopover as a base to explore nearby regions stemmed from past family experiences living abroad for extended periods. These postings, in places like Riyadh, Saudi Arabia, and Montreal, Canada, highlighted the benefits of having a base for a few years, allowing for immersion in the local community and short trips from that location. It is a low-stress way of traveling that fosters deeper connections with the local culture.

Living Like a Local in Valencia:
During my stay in Valencia, an apartment was rented in the heart of the ancient city, surrounded by festive streets. Exploring the winding lanes, people-watching in cafes, and enjoying serenades from strolling musicians made each day a rich cultural experience. Day trips and various social activities provided further opportunities to connect with locals and build a social network.

A Sense of Home:
While living in Spain, there was a brief trip to Morocco for visa reasons. Upon returning to

Valencia, there was a profound sense of coming "home". Familiarity and the comfort of a well-established local network made the return feel like a warm embrace.

Continuous Choices in Travel:
A key principle in travel is that you face daily decisions about where to go and what to explore. The fear of missing out on unchosen paths is a common dilemma. Regardless of the path you choose, it's up to you to embrace it fully and turn it into a memorable experience. Your attitude and approach play a significant role in how each choice shapes your overall travel experience.

Summary:
Living like a local provides an opportunity for authentic cultural experiences that go beyond what traditional tourists or independent travellers might encounter. The key is to engage with the local community and participate in activities from day one, opening doors to new experiences and meaningful connections with people and cultures.

Chapter 29
Living Like a Local

Accommodation and Cultural Immersion:

The choice of accommodation plays a significant role in experiencing life as a local. For the author, the apartment chosen in the heart of an ancient city was essential to the cultural experience. Living amidst the local community, being surrounded by cultural elements, and even struggling with local pronunciations were all part of the immersive experience. However, for a more extended stay, beachside apartments might be a preferable choice.

Balancing Expat Clusters:
While staying close to clusters of expatriates can offer a sense of familiarity and comfort, it may distract from fully appreciating the local culture.

Balancing the need for comfort with a desire for cultural immersion is key.

Cost-Effective Extended Stays:
The cost-effectiveness of short-term rental accommodations increases with the length of stay. For extended periods, you might find yourself paying a rent like the value you'd receive if you rented your home property or what you'd pay in rent. Daily living expenses can be comparable to those at home, depending on your dining and travel choices. This allows you to live like a local on a local's budget with only an airfare needed to get there.

Choosing Accommodation:
If living like a local is part of your travel plan, researching and booking accommodation in advance can be beneficial. Real estate agents, Airbnb, and homestays are readily accessible sources. House swaps, house-sitting arrangements, and local referrals are added options. For solo travellers, the choice of pre-booking or looking after arrival depends on personal preferences.

Routines in Unfamiliar Places:
Upon arriving in a new destination, you're excited to escape your old routines. However, it's intriguing how people quickly establish new routines. Finding shortcuts to the supermarket, finding favourite dining spots, and creating daily habits are all part of the human instinct to turn the unfamiliar into the familiar. These newly established routines become as comforting as those at home, and this might signal that it's time to move on to the next place!

Summary:
Living like a local can help you minimize costs and integrate into a new culture. It offers an opportunity to embrace the local way of life and routines. The longer you stay in a place, the more your daily living costs can align with local budgets, making it a cost-effective way to explore the world while truly immersing yourself in local cultures.

THE YOUTHFUL MIDLIFE TRAVELLER

Chapter 30
Living Like a Local Summary

Committing to a Single Place:

The idea of traveling to a destination and committing to staying in one place for an extended period, purely for the experience, may seem challenging. It's different from traveling from place to place, where each new destination provides constant stimulation.

Challenges and Rewards:
Committing to a single place can initially present challenges, such as the time it takes to form new friendships. However, the rewards are fulfilling. It offers a unique form of travel that could be described as a low-burnout style. Choosing a location with a

THE YOUTHFUL MIDLIFE TRAVELLER

community of permanent expatriates can make social integration more accessible, especially if you don't speak the local language.

Getting Involved:
The secret to maximizing the experience of living like a local is to engage in local activities right from the start. Participating in activities is a way to make friends and become an active part of the community.

A Base to Call Home:
Having a base allows you to explore not only the local culture but also take short trips from that location. Your base becomes a place where you feel at home, and it's where you can reunite with new friends. These friendships can be long-lasting and part of your life, no matter where your next adventure takes you.

Select Few for Fulfillment:
Given that it's impossible to experience every country on the planet, choosing just a few destinations and immersing yourself in the local culture can provide a deeply fulfilling travel experience.

KEEPING YOUR DREAM ALIVE

Here's some closing thoughts and words of encouragement to help you maintain enthusiasm for pursuing your travel dreams. Here are the key takeaways:

1. Solo Travel:
Do not to wait for a travel partner. Solo traveling is a fantastic alternative and offers unique experiences. Many solo women travellers embark on remarkable journeys.

2. Partnered Travel:

While solo travellers have the motivation to meet new people, partnered travellers can also have an adventure of a lifetime. Traveling together creates memories that can be cherished for years.

3. Slow-Paced Experience:

The type of travel discussed in this guide, focused on experience and immersion, offers a more relaxed and fulfilling experience compared to busy, pre-planned itineraries.

4. Overcoming Inner Obstacles:

The biggest challenge in pursuing our dreams is often ourselves. Our inner voices may try to keep us in our comfort zones, but it's essential to confront and address those fears. Taking baby steps and gradually expanding your comfort zone can be a successful approach.

5. Embracing Challenges:

Challenging oneself is essential for personal growth. It's a reminder that there's still plenty of life to live, even in midlife. The worst outcome is that your grand idea might not work out, but it's better to try and fail than to regret not trying at all.

6. The Power of Commitment:

The need to commit to following your heart, is best summarised in a quote by William Hutchison Murray:

*"**Until one is committed**, there is hesitancy, the chance to draw back, always ineffectiveness. Concerning all acts of initiative and creation, there is one elementary truth the ignorance of which kills countless ideas and splendid plans: that the moment one commits oneself, then providence moves too..."*

It's now your turn to make your travel dreams a reality. Embrace the opportunity and embark on your journey to explore, experience, and enrich your life through travel.

Make it happen. Happy travels. You deserve it!

ABOUT THE AUTHOR

Chris Herrmann has drawn upon a unique life journey to bring you this insightful guide. His personal odyssey encompasses a life anchored in family, career, and community engagement. With a successful corporate management background, he was content in his business, time spent with family, travel adventures, and active participation in community projects.

However, a profound turning point arose when his wife of forty years lost her life to cancer. Chris realized that life's unpredictable turns are not reserved for others but can dramatically alter our own path. He faced the challenge of navigating a future without his life partner and decided to step beyond his comfort zone.

In search of personal growth and transformation,

THE YOUTHFUL MIDLIFE TRAVELLER

Chris embarked on a remarkable twelve-month backpacking adventure around the world. This decision was no simple feat. It required him to confront an array of fears, including the fear of the unknown and the emotional strain of leaving behind his family and the familiar comforts of home.

His global adventure took him across 23 countries and led him to sleep in 123 different places. Along the way, he discovered captivating destinations and met a diverse array of people. His encounters spanned a spectrum of experiences, from the enthralling to the eye-opening.

Upon returning from this transformative journey, Chris was left with one resounding question: why should the younger generation have all the fun? He observed that younger Travellers embraced adventure, exploration, and cultural immersion with unwavering confidence. Chris was motivated to inspire his own generation, encouraging them to embrace the joys of travel and the life-changing experiences it can bring.

Drawing upon his wealth of experiences, his introspective insights, and the lessons learned during his travels, Chris has penned this guide to inspire others. It is a testament to his unwavering belief that life's adventures should be accessible to everyone, regardless of age or life stage. Through this book, he aims to empower individuals to embrace the exhilarating opportunities for personal growth and fulfillment that travel can offer.

RESOURCES

In addition to this book, an exclusive online resource provides an and comprehensive source of additional relevant travel information.

This includes links and video interviews of other independent travellers. Access to a video (and audio) version of the book provides an exciting way to visualise travel opportunities. An invitation to an online travel group offers an opportunity to share and learn from other travellers.

To access Resources, please go to:
youthfulmidlifetravel.com/resources.

THE YOUTHFUL MIDLIFE TRAVELLER

www.ingramcontent.com/pod-product-compliance
Lightning Source LLC
Chambersburg PA
CBHW050315010526
44107CB00055B/2247